ENGAGING POST-CHRISTIAN CULTURE: OUR MISSION IN A NEW CONTEXT

There was a time when Christianity was at the center of society. When most people grew up attending church. When Christians held influence in the public square and were viewed as credible in culture. When America was still thought of as a "Christian nation." Not so anymore.

We live in post-Christian context. And while Christians could bemoan this reality, it's not all bad news. The end of the Christian America dream is the beginning of a new opportunity. A chance for following Jesus to not be defined by heritage, by politics, or by cultural convenience. An opportunity for the church to be an authentic light, a countercultural example, a curious and winsome presence in a broken world.

But it won't be easy. The way forward is unfamiliar (to us at least). And there are risks involved. In this Q Society Room experience, your group will be challenged to explore the dynamics of a post-Christian culture and imagine our mission in a new context.

ENGAGING POST-CHRISTIAN CULTURE

WELCOME

WELCOME TO THE SOCIETY ROOM

Q Society Room studies are a new, yet historic way to consider issues of faith and culture in the context of a group learning environment. The Society Rooms of the late 1600s and the Clapham Circle of the early 1800s are riveting examples of small gatherings of leaders that would convene, dialogue, learn, and work together to renew their culture. Consider the impact of these early Society Rooms:

In 1673 Dr. Anthony Horneck, a Church of England minister in London, preached a number of what he called "awakening sermons." As a result several young men began to meet together weekly in order to build up one another in the Christian faith. They gathered in small groups at certain fixed locations and their places of meeting became known as Society Rooms. In these gatherings they read the Bible, studied religious books and prayed; they also went out among the poor to relieve want at their own expense and to show kindness to all. By

1730 nearly one hundred of these Societies existed in London, and others—perhaps another hundred—were to be found in cities and towns throughout England. The Societies movement became, in many senses, the cradle of the Revival ..." (Arnold Dallimore, *George Whitefield*, Vol. 1, Crossway, 1990, pp. 28–29)

Following this historical example, this group study is designed to renew your minds as leaders so that you can make a difference in society. Society Room communities like yours are characterized by a commitment to put learning into action. And no doubt, over the course of the next few weeks, your innermost beliefs and preconceived ideas about life, faith, the world, and your cultural responsibility will be challenged. But that's the point.

Here's how it works. Your group will gather five times to discuss important topics related to the overall theme of this study. Sometimes you'll be

given something to do or read before your group gathers. It's important for you to take these "assignments" seriously. They won't demand much time, but they will require intentionality. Doing these things ahead of time will cultivate a richer and more stimulating group experience as you begin to practice what you are learning.

For each group gathering, set aside about one hour and fifteen minutes for the discussion in a place with minimal distractions. Your group may want to share a meal together first, but be sure to allow enough time for unhurried dialogue to take place. Sometimes you'll watch a short video. But conversation and dialogue will always be the priority. The leader of the group will not teach or lecture, but instead will ask questions, facilitate conversation, and seek input from everyone. Be prepared to ask good questions and share your own thoughts. Sometimes you'll even debate an issue by taking sides and thinking through all the complexities. The goal of each gathering is for your group to be stimulated by a particular idea and learn together as you discuss its impact on your faith, your lives, and culture in general. Your group may not arrive at a consensus regarding any given topic. That's okay. Be respectful of others, even when you disagree with them. We can learn something from everyone.

Before your fifth gathering, you will undertake a group project together. You may be tempted to skip this. Don't! Your group project might be the most important part of your experience. Genuine learning as a community takes place when you engage the ideas you are discussing and do something together as a group.

In the end, be committed to this group and the learning process that is about to ensue. Your willingness to prepare for group gatherings, keep an open mind, and demonstrate eagerness to learn together will pave the way for a great experience.

YOUR PLACE IN CULTURE

INTRODUCTIONS

At the beginning of your first gathering, spend about fifteen minutes introducing yourselves to one another and discussing your channel of cultural influence.

There are several different social institutions that touch every person in a given society. These areas of influence contain most of the industries and organizations that consistently shape our culture. They touch every aspect of our lives, and most of us find our vocational roles in one or more of these areas. They are the seven channels of cultural influence.

As you begin your Society Room experience, you'll notice that most, if not all, of these channels are represented in your group. Start your first gathering by sharing which particular channel of influence you participate in. Give the rest of the group a sense of how your channel contributes to shaping society in general. Then, throughout the rest of the group experience, reflect on how your learning will affect the channel to which you've been called.

Channels of Cultural Influence

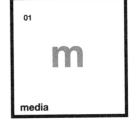

01

m

media

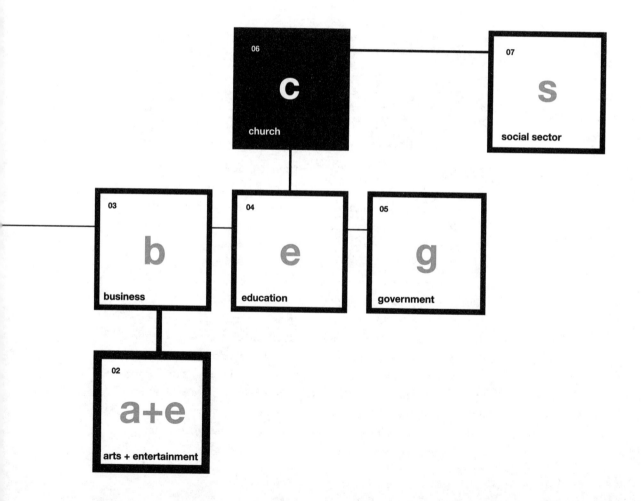

—

ROUNDTABLE DISCUSSIONS

As part of this Q Society Room, we convened leaders from various channels of culture to discuss these important topics. Throughout the study, you will be introduced to their thoughts and ideas in hopes of stirring your conversation and dialogue.

Gabe Lyons
Q Founder & Author
Gabe Lyons is the author of *The Next Christians: The Good News About the End of Christian America* and the creator of Q — a learning community that educates Christians on their responsibility and opportunities to renew culture. Lyons coauthored *UnChristian*, a bestselling book that reveals exclusive research on pop culture's negative perception of Christians. Gabe, his wife Rebekah, and their three children reside in Atlanta, Georgia.

Dave Gibbons
Pastor & Social Entrepreneur
Dave is the founding pastor of NewSong, a multi-site international third-culture church. He is an innovative strategist and cultural specialist with global experience in the arts, business, church, and community development. Dave is on the board of World Vision US and founder and chief visionary officer of Xealot, a strategic innovations group, creatively connecting resources to leaders around the world.

Shane Hipps

Technology & Faith Author

Shane is Lead Pastor of Trinity Mennonite Church. Before accepting his call as a pastor, he was a strategic planner in advertising where he worked on the multimillion-dollar communications plan for Porsche. It was here that he gained expertise in understanding media and culture. Shane is the author of *Flickering Pixels* and *The Hidden Power of Electronic Culture: How Media Shapes Faith, The Gospel, and Church.*

Debra Hirsch

Writer & Cultural Observer

Debra is an Aussie living in America. She is a minister at the Tribe of L.A., an eclectic bunch of missional artists and vagabonds who meet in downtown Los Angeles. She also serves on the leadership team of Christian Associates International, a church-planting agency into three continents.

Darren Whitehead

Pastor, Chicago

Darren currently serves as a Teaching Pastor at Willow Creek Community Church. He also leads the Next Gen Ministries and the Creative Arts departments. Prior to Willow Creek, Darren served as Teaching Pastor and Director of Student Ministries at The People's Church in Nashville, Tennessee.

Everything is fine, but the ship is still heading in the wrong direction.

EDWARD DE BONO

One of the peculiar sins of the twentieth century, which we've developed to a very high level, is the sin of credulity. It has been said that when human beings stop believing in God they believe in nothing. The truth is much worse: they believe in anything.

MALCOLM MUGGERIDGE

[People] make history, and not the other way around. In periods where there is no leadership, society stands still. Progress occurs when courageous, skillful leaders seize the opportunity to change things for the better.

HARRY TRUMAN

GROUP GATHERING ONE

A NEW MISSION TO THE WEST

THE WORLD IS DIFFERENT

DISCUSS

Take a few minutes and share with the rest of the group how you believe the world has changed the most in recent memory.

The world is changing; it always has been. Every generation has broken new ground. Cultural shifts are always reforming the landscape. The past has always seemed outdated. Indeed, it's been said that the only constant in our world is change. All the same, massive changes have taken place in Western culture in the last hundred years that seem to overshadow all others in history. And the world around us is totally different.

DISCUSSION STARTERS

What are the biggest changes that have taken place in culture over your or your parents' lifetime?

How has technology transformed our lives?

What have the effects of these cultural changes been on Christianity?

OPINIONS OF TECHNILOGICAL AND SOCIAL CHANGES

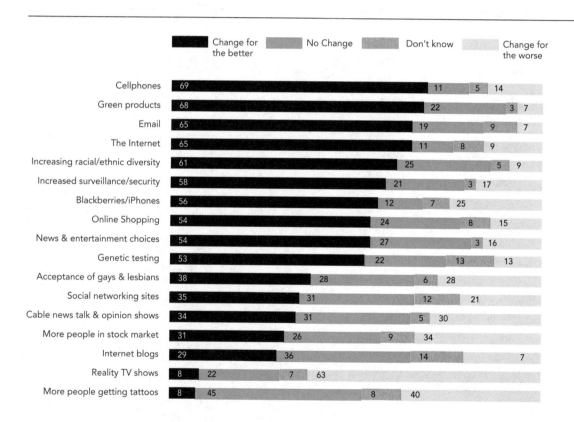

Source: Pew Research Center for the People & the Press: "Public Looks Back at Worst Decade in 50 Years Internet, Cell Phones Are Changes for the Better," December 21, 2009 at http://pewresearch.org/pubs/1447/worst-decade-major-technological-communications-advances.

A NEW MISSION TO THE WEST

WATCH

View Q Talk: Third Mission to the West by Os Guinness.

Record your thoughts on the talk on page 17.

Os Guinness is a philosopher and social critic who has written or edited more than twenty-five books, including *The Call*, *Time for Truth*, *Long Journey Home*, and his latest book, *The Case for Civility—And Why Our Future Depends on It*.

At Q New York, Os Guinness outlined the colossal changes that have taken place and how they threaten our faith, both from the inside and outside. In this presentation, he describes the most pressing cultural issues we face and offers helpful insights concerning the way forward for the church today.

—

"Our challenge with any cultural change is to discern it, to assess it, and to engage it."

—

"Our world is as furiously religious as ever . . . a fearsome friction of more worldviews clashing with other worldviews than the world has ever seen. And we have to live with repercussions of this at many levels."

—

"We have to win people, and not win battles."

—

"The three tasks we have are: first, to restore the integrity of the faith; second, to restore the credibility of the gospel to educated, thinking people; and third, to restore civility in public life."

THOUGHTS

THE FOCUS OF OUR MESSAGE

DEBATE

Split the group into two sides* and spend fifteen minutes debating the issue:

Are you optimistic that Christians can turn the tide and reengage American culture in such a way that the gospel regains credibility? Or, are you largely pessimistic, believing that Christianity will continue to be marginalized in America?

Record your thoughts on each position on pages 20-21.

Use the following debate starters to guide your time.

The church faces numerous complex challenges in our post-Christian world. Os Guinness outlined the philosophical roots of these challenges and suggested we have done a poor job of assessing them and responding effectively.

Are you optimistic that Christians can turn the tide and reengage American culture in such a way that the gospel regains its credibility? Or, are you largely pessimistic, believing that Christianity will continue to be marginalized in America?

DEBATE STARTERS

Is secularization an unstoppable force in our culture?

Can Christianity ever have a meaningful influence in a post-Christian culture?

What do failed attempts to legislate morality (e.g., abortion) reveal about our ability to influence culture in the political realm?

Where should we place our hope: in Christ's power to transform individual lives or Christ's power to transform entire cultures?

Even if you don't agree with the side you are representing, consider and offer the best arguments for your position. Be respectful.

—

YES

I'm optimistic that Christians can continue to impact Western culture and the gospel can regain its credibility.

THOUGHTS

—

NO

I'm pessimistic that Christians can have any positive effect on the wider culture; our best hope is to convert those who are willing to listen to the gospel.

THOUGHTS

BEING A BLESSING

REFLECT

Have a few people in your group take turns reading this section aloud.

Then journal your thoughts on pages 24-25.

Genesis 12:1–3 describes the calling and mission that God gave to Abraham. And not only to Abraham, but to all his descendants—the ethnic nation of Israel and also us, the spiritual "children of Abraham" (Gal. 3:7–17). Consider this pivotal vision:

> The Lord had said to Abram, "Go from your country, your people and your father's household to the land I will show you.
>
> "I will make you into a great nation,
>   and I will bless you;
> I will make your name great,
>   and you will be a blessing.
> I will bless those who bless you,
>   and whoever curses you I will curse;
>   and all peoples on earth
> will be blessed through you."
> – Genesis 12:1–3

Biblical scholar Christopher Wright discusses the significance of this passage:

Genesis 12:1–3 is pivotal in the book of Genesis: it moves the story forward from the preceding eleven chapters, which record God's dealings with all the nations (sometimes called "the primeval history"), into the patriarchal narratives that lead to the emergence of Israel as a distinct nation. And it is pivotal in the whole Bible because it does exactly what Paul says—it "announces the gospel in advance." That is, it declares the good news that in spite of all we have read in Genesis 1–11, it is God's ultimate purpose to bless humanity (which is very good news indeed by the time you reach Gen. 11). And the story of how that blessing for all nations has come about occupies the rest of the Bible, with Christ as the central focus. Indeed the closing vision of the canon, with people of every tribe and nation and language worshiping the living God (Rev. 7:9–10), clearly echoes the promise of Genesis 12:3 and binds the whole story together.

The whole Bible could be portrayed as a very long answer to a very simple question: What can God do about the sin and rebellion of the human race? Genesis 12 through Revelation 22 is God's answer to the question posed by the bleak narratives of Genesis 3–11. Or in terms of the overall argument of this book, Genesis 3–11 sets the problem that the mission of God addresses from Genesis 12 to Revelation 22. (*The Mission of God*, IVP Academic, 2006, pp. 194–195)

REFLECTION STARTERS

Spend a few minutes journaling your thoughts to the two questions below. Then, share your reflections with the group.

What does it mean for the people of God to "be a blessing"?

How should Christians recover this mission of being God's blessing when it comes to engaging with "secular" culture in our own day?

JOURNAL

JOURNAL

—

OUR POSTURE TOWARD CULTURE

CONCLUDE

—

There was a time when Christianity dominated Western culture. But now we live in a culture that is increasingly pluralistic and even more hostile toward the claims of Christianity. We must rethink our overall posture toward culture and recover our ultimate goal: to bring God's redemption and restoration to our culture by being a blessing.

What does it mean for you specifically to "be a blessing" in your cultural channel of influence?

—

RENEWING CITIES THROUGH MISSIONAL TRIBES

PREPARE FOR NEXT GATHERING

—

Before your next gathering, read the Q Short by Jon Tyson beginning on page 30. Be sure to set aside some uninterrupted time for this. Try not to save it until the last minute. When you read the essay, underline, highlight, or jot down comments about ideas that are particularly interesting, disconcerting, or challenging. Be prepared to share why at the next gathering.

RENEWING CITIES THROUGH MISSIONAL TRIBES

RENEWING CITIES THROUGH MISSIONAL TRIBES

By Jon Tyson

I first met Anna when she came to our apartment for a church group. An actress, waitress, and recovering alcoholic, she was desperate to find her place in the city. She came back week after week to sit through our Bible study and worship time. When I asked her why she bothered to return, it was as if she struggled to articulate the motive in her heart. Eventually she responded with, "I guess I was hoping to find somewhere to belong." Hundreds of miles from her family, pursuing her second or third "life dream," she articulated the sense of angst that in many ways defines this generation: "I'm just pretty lonely and struggle to find people I can trust." Interestingly enough, Anna was not a Christian, not even close, yet was willing to endure the "Jesus time" to simply be around people who seemed vaguely interested in her life.

I have heard versions of this story dozens of times.

From Wall Street traders to advertising executives, from nannies to MTV producers, it seems that in some fundamental way we are incurably communal. What's ironic is that all of these people are living in New York City, surrounded by millions of people, yet feeling incredibly alone.

Though they may feel like it, these people are not alone. This loss of community has in some ways become our collective experience of American life. This relational disconnection was first identified and popularized in the year 2000 in Robert Putnam's work *Bowling Alone*.[1] Simply put, he proposed that America was losing its sense of community, or its social capital—the reality that we are a part of "the whole," and that we participate in small but significant ways to the greater good. He noticed "that we sign fewer petitions, belong to fewer organizations that meet, know our neighbors less, meet with friends less frequently,

and even socialize with our families less often."[2] Putnam went on to suggest that changes in work, family structure, age, suburban life, television, computers, women's roles, and other factors have contributed to this decline.

If Putnam is right, this loss of connection poses both opportunities and challenges for the church at large. A loss of cultural connection strikes at the heart of our faith: it hinders our ability to share the gospel in organic, relational ways and makes it difficult to know and serve our neighbors. Conversely, it creates a desire for a loving, accepting community to those who are disillusioned, disconnected, and alone. So, how can the church position itself to be a community of love in this emerging culture of disconnection, and will our popular small group programs really be enough to engage this decline? Moreover, are there other trends that we have overlooked that could offer us some clues as to how the church could function as a catalyst for authentic community that is also missional? I believe there are.

SOCIAL CAPITAL

First, let's consider the purported loss of social capital in society. Our social ties have value like any other kind of capital—financial, human, or physical—and those connections that we take for granted create a kind of relational wealth that we are not always aware of. Within the overlapping networks in our lives, we both find and contribute to a richness of community value. Thus, social capital is a trust that arises from our community of relationships that enables us to help others in mutually beneficial ways. Put another way, social capital acts as both sociological superglue to keep us connected and sociological WD-40 to facilitate interaction.

With this in mind, Putnam defines social capital as:

> ... those tangible substances [that] count for most in the daily lives of people: namely good will, fellowship, sympathy, and social intercourse among the individuals and families who make up a social unit ... The individual is helpless socially, if left to himself. ... If he comes into contact with his neighbor, and they with other neighbors, there will be an accumulation of social capital, which may immediately satisfy his social needs and which may bear a social potentiality sufficient to improvement of living conditions in the whole community.[3]

So where does social capital come from? Social capital is the overflow effect of three things in our lives.

1. Our networks. These are the people that we are connected to in the overlapping segments of our lives. This could be the parents from a child's soccer team, our neighbors, a study group or local book club, or people from a class we are currently taking.

2. Our norms. This is the flow and rhythm of our lives, our habits and social reflexes, our patterns, behaviors, and daily interactions: where we shop, what we do with our leisure time, our schools, places of employment, and the maps we subconsciously follow that we have created over time. This could best be described as "our way of life."

3. Our values. These are the things that matter to us, what we fight for, organize around, give to, get involved with, and care about.

When these three things overlap in the right degree, a new element is released into the fabric of these interactions called social capital. This is a shared sense of trust and a desire to help one another. This in turn lets us be a part of a newly established "us," which creates a new sense of belonging. This is what gives us that sense of community, safety, and place, and what makes our lives so rich.

We all know what it feels like to chat with a neighbor in an elevator and catch up on local gossip, or go to a local coffee shop to sit in "our seat." All of us have sensed social capital being released when bumping into someone at the store or finding out you share something in common with those at school. It's these interactions, these "me too" moments that work as small deposits and contact points, which over time accumulate and increase our sociological wealth.

When these interactions disappear from our lives, there doesn't seem to be a difference at first, as in a next-door neighbor moving away, or dropping out of a club or team, but if this continues, the cumulative effect over time creates a real sense of loss. If all the neighbors you know move away, and the local shops you frequent are replaced by chain stores, and your neighbors are replaced by others with vastly different values, then the loss of capital is really felt. Your networks have disbanded, your normal flow of life is disrupted, and there are few around you that share your values.

Putnam's observations are most visible today through a discernable loss of participation in official, organized communities. People change employers and residences at an alarming rate,

and don't seem to make the same connections they used to. With longer work hours, demanding schedules, and long hours spent commuting, our collective sense of community is dissolving—

join groups in their workplaces, or re-up for civic institutions are all solid starting points. But is this enough?

SOCIETY SEEMS TO HAVE FRAGMENTED SUCH THAT EVEN THE IDEAS AND INSTITUTIONS THAT WE ARE CALLED BACK TO ARE FUNDAMENTALLY CHARACTERIZED BY INDIVIDUALISM.

not completely, but substantially. Without the sociological glue and WD-40 we need, this loss of social capital could do real damage to our lives.

In order to restore this cultural capital and community to our world, Putnam suggests that we need to help integrate people's lives back into the official social structures of the culture. These social structures form a sort of frame around which culture is built, and around which we can rebuild our communities. This solution is noble and thoughtful; asking people to shorten their commutes to work, watch less TV, carpool,

For example, Putnam states, "Let us find ways to ensure that by 2010 the level of civic engagement among Americans then coming of age in all parts of our society will match that of their grandparents when they were that same age, and that at the same time bridging social capital will be substantially greater than it was in their grandparents' era."[4] This is commendable. However, society seems to have fragmented such that even the ideas and institutions that we are called back to are fundamentally characterized by individualism—so much so that participating in them often feels like engaging with social cannibals, rather than other

contributors. We have all had experiences that were intended to create community, which ended up leaving us feeling exhausted and drained, instead of refreshed.

Another problem is that we have no allegiance to a civic whole, no metanarrative, or any real connection with our grandparents. We don't know how they lived or have any real understanding of their times and challenges. Many of us simply have no models to work from, guides to follow, or vision to move toward. We cannot go back to a way of life we are so thoroughly removed from.

SOCIAL CAPITAL AND THE CHURCH

In the midst of this cultural fragmentation, the church has tried to address the problem by calling people to a vision of *true* community. But no matter how hard we try, the cultural forces are often too powerful and persuasive to counteract. We are barely different from our culture—busy, driven, individualistic, and disconnected—and so, we too have lost our social capital. Our lives also lack that mystical missing ingredient. We have become cultural consumers who no longer have the networks, norms, or values for anything other than our own peace and affluence. It shouldn't be this way. As people who are called to be a new and different kind of community—a city on a hill— we should offer something toward the common good and the renewal of our world. But because our schedules, practices, values, and networks are often identical to those who are not believers, we lack the ability to offer them anything different than the fragmenting forces they are already encountering in society. We have somehow forgotten that we are called to something bigger than our own fulfillment and dreams.

PROGRAMMED COMMUNITY OFTEN FEELS LIKE A SMALL GROUP VERSION OF EHARMONY.

Church leaders have become aware of this problem. We've recognized the importance of social capital and its connection to spreading the gospel, and we've scrambled to bridge the gaps in our fragmented culture. The primary way we have done this is through small group ministry. The general idea is to invite people back together by organizing them in ways that let them connect around the main needs of their lives. For many, this has been an interesting experience. Programming community based on demographics may help

people connect, but it often fails to help people in the areas of their norms and values. We can create "a church network" (small group) but many struggle to integrate this weekly-programmed event into the norms, values, and other networks of their lives.

Despite its good intentions, programmed community often feels like a small group version of eHarmony. Fill out a life stage/felt needs profile and you are matched up with other people at a similar stage of life and loneliness with the hope that it all works out. Different communities have had varying degrees of success with this approach, but for the cynics outside the church, this is hardly different from what is available in the world. And these inward-facing, needs-based groups often fail to take into consideration the kingdom of God at large.

Many churches with small group ministries are now publicly vocalizing this angst. They are coming to the conclusion that traditional small group ministry has too often done little to impact the way people actually live or reorient their lives around the kingdom of God. I believe success has been limited in the small group approach because it fails to address at least two of the deeper realities of our lives.

Time. People's lives are now centered on their jobs, leisure activities, and families, and this inward vision is reinforced by millions of marketing messages each year. Therefore, we must wrestle with this question: how can we get people to care about the greater good, when we don't have a shared commitment to anything greater than our own careers and shrinking leisure time? People have lost their allegiance to the church's vision if it doesn't help fulfill their own, and in an ever competitive workplace requiring longer and longer hours, personal time becomes the highest commodity. People simply can't center their busy lives on official church programs anymore.

Trust. Another concern for leaders has been the distrust of authority and disillusionment with the institutional church. It seems that no matter how hard church leaders try, or what the latest conference offers, it's extremely hard to get people to believe that the church knows best. Combine that with the heartbreaking hypocrisy of exposed national leaders, and you have a real problem. When cynicism and secularism are the framing narrative of culture, getting people to center their lives on officially established programs under official church authority is increasingly hard. Moreover, because the church has been ostracized by the culture and pushed to the fringe of society, to call people to deep involvement in an institution that is so disconnected means we have to pull them further away from engaging in the networks, norms, and values that actually make up their lives.

PEOPLE ARE UTILIZING NEW
TECHNOLOGIES, SCHEDULES, AND
FREEDOMS TO FORM ORGANIC CAPITAL
AMONG THEMSELVES.

Perhaps the biggest problem with the programmed approach is that it can cause real disconnects with our mission. If people only have social networks, norms, and values that interact inside the church, then we cannot connect meaningfully with the culture at large. This leaves us radically disconnected. We can unintentionally isolate people from the greater community and become so desperate to "connect" that we sever other organic relationships that allow the gospel to flow from one life to another. In essence, we lose the ability to be salt and light. We lose kingdom opportunities in networks, norms, and values that let us be a voice of an alternative vision to the world.

Anna, the actress, waitress, and recovering alcoholic, eventually became a Christian, and her passion for connection in the church was contagious. She served in the children's ministry, got involved in a small group, and even came to church early to greet new people. At coffee recently, she expressed her concern that something seemed to be missing. All of these programs were still rooted within the confines of her small church network and didn't overlap with the other parts of her life. She was also struggling to live the values of Jesus out in the "real world" and in other networks of friends. It was like there was a giant disconnect between her church world and the rest of the world. While pouring out her thoughts on this, she said something to the effect of, "We simply cannot love one another as Jesus

commanded, if our lives only overlap in fifteen-minute segments before and after programmed Christian events. And we cannot reach out to those far from God if the normal flow of our lives is disconnected from theirs and channeled into church programs. It's like God calls us to life together, to the weaving of the fabric and moments of our lives, so the expression of the kingdom becomes a reality in our midst, rather than a idea in our heads."

What Anna wants to be a part of is an integrated life, a recovering of social capital, but with a missional twist—where her networks and norms and values are infused with the reality of Jesus. As a pastor, I have heard this reaction many times, and it has led me to believe that our culture has undergone such profound shifts in community that another great program to manufacture relationships is not the answer. Perhaps the key lies in the nature of the shifts themselves.

URBAN TRIBES:
SHIFTING SOCIAL CAPITAL

Several years after *Bowling Alone* came out, and several small group programming attempts later, I came across a book that reflected and responded to these ideas in some fresh and insightful ways: *Urban Tribes: A Generation Redefines Friendship, Family and Commitment* by Ethan Watters.[5] It challenged the assumption that cultural capital would be recovered through official institutions

and efforts, and suggested instead, that it may reorganize through unofficial communities he called urban tribes. Watters, a single, never-married San Franciscan, observed how this sense of trust, community, and belonging—this social capital—was all around him, but in less formal social networks that were becoming the new superglue of our time.

As Watters surveyed his community and city, he noticed that his was a rich relational world of high social capital, and that his tribe had a deep sense of community. There was a real sense of belonging and desire to help each other in mutually beneficial ways. Although disconnected from the previous generation's traditional structures and official civic institutions, people were utilizing new technologies, schedules, and freedoms to form organic capital among themselves.

Others are noticing the phenomenon as well. Journalist Howard Fineman highlights the cultural and ethnic dimensions: "As neighborhoods and schools become more diverse, marriages become more mixed, and social hierarchies break down, old lines are getting blurry. Voluntary tribes are a way of re-creating a sense of community."[6] So what is an urban tribe? And is this a sociological opportunity for the church to consider?

Urban tribes are the social networks of friends we build in and around cities. They often consist of people who are single well into their twenties and thirties and who form a new kind of family unity that functions like traditional families used to, in terms of support and structure. Each tribe builds its own culture over time, through weekly rituals, shared history, language, insider jokes, weekend trips, and relational support. They screen potential mates, loan each other money, provide housing help, and even start businesses together.

These tribes owe their existence to some of the major shifts that in many ways frame this generation.

1. Displacement. People are moving from their places of birth to college, then cities, and then other cities to pursue careers in industry centers and rarely resettling in their places of origin.

2. Freedom. People are getting married later than any generation in American history and have less family responsibility than either parents or grandparents. Their time and resources are primarily for themselves.

3. Causes. People are aware and concerned about the needs of their world, and *the* world, like never before. Fineman notes: "More than 'associations'... these [tribes] are emotionally intense affinity groups based on shared aims, obsessions or political

crusades, not on DNA."[7]

4. Loneliness. This loss of family, displacement, freedom, and need converge to create a hunger for community that is greater than their parents.

Watters explains the intersection of these factors:

We live further away from our kinship networks. We're not joining community groups. ... [We are] a group that is freer than any generation I can imagine. Because freedom is a lack of restraints, we don't often look at what freedom is. We're free of parenting responsibilities. That means that we have a lot of free time. We're also free of parental control. There's a corollary to that parental role. Other advice givers have stepped away from the plate. There aren't the mentors, priests, bosses, and other strict advice givers. Now they just encourage us and offer support. They had a tough time, so they don't have a unified front to give us advice. We're also free of punishment for the consequences of our actions. We're no longer disciplined by our elders. We have this notion that we've gone to the city once to create ourselves, and that we can always go to another city and try again. We also have more dating and relationship options. There's also no order in which we're

expected to live our lives. Free from general social strife. There's no shared sense of our being born for some specific purpose.[8]

Anna is the perfect example: free and open, looking to connect, but struggling to make it happen, especially as it relates to church. For those like Anna, a generation suspicious of "official" community, joining your local club or civic group feels more like an act of sheer desperation than a plausible response to the need to belong. That's why Christian attempts to program community can feel forced at best and coercive at worst.

Our culture offers several examples of the urban tribe in popular media, some of which we even emulate for community. Consider the shows *Seinfeld*, *Sex and the City*, and *Friends*. People from different parts of the country, coming together to form a new family unit, with rituals and taboos and customs and language, all happening organically, unofficially, and in many ways, powerfully (even when we know it's just TV). These shows highlight overlapping networks, personal values, and the norms in life. *Seinfeld* was even able to build entire themes and episodes on the minutest details of life's norms. The people in these shows don't seem to need anything official to function well together. Indeed, they often reject official structures. Imagine asking Carrie to join a small group at your church, or the cast of *Seinfeld* to join the Lions Club. You get the point.

It appears that Watters and others have been able to understand and describe one of the primary ways our culture is reforming in light of recent cultural fragmentation. These tribes seem to transcend class, race, past, and experience and have a unique ability to weave life together in such a way that social capital is powerfully released. Urban tribes may be the new glue and WD-40 of our time.

As a pastor working with literally hundreds of these late-to-marry twenty and thirty somethings, I have found these tribal observations to be true. There is a deep loneliness and longing to belong, but informally, and in ways the church has not traditionally offered. And it makes me wonder: what if we could harness these tribes into some sort of missional movements in the city? What if tribes not only connected, but also served, and helped generate capital through our cities and networks? What if the key to recovering social capital wasn't through official cultural institutions, or church programs, but by calling people to a new vision of community through the medium of the urban tribe?

I KNOW, I KNOW

At this point, some may be cynical that informal urban tribes can offer any hope for restoring social capital and creating common good, let alone become a foundational community through which God can release kingdom renewal into our world.

But consider this: culture today is rarely formed around official institutions, but rather through varying networks of trusted friends through whom we share experiences, relationships, ideas, successes, failures, celebrations, and milestones. These urban tribes could be the most natural and trusted way the gospel can move through a city. When I reflect on the way we have planted and grown our church in New York, it has almost exclusively been through tribes. We haven't done any marketing, handed out any freebies, or begged people to come to our services. Almost everyone who has been reached through our church has been reached through tribal groups. People still show up as individuals, but increasingly they are showing up together, community already formed, seeking to infuse Christian spirituality into an already existing network. These loose, interconnected networks often have surprising reach in a given community, with each tribe literally cross-pollinating with dozens of other members of other tribes. These networks spread through the relational fabric of New York and filter into almost every social category and industry imaginable. Watters' thoughts about tribal connections across a city seem to be coming true:

> How might these urban tribes form a network across a city? These networks rely heavily on weak ties … the shadow ties, people we don't know yet, but people who will come into our lives within a year. Certainly, when I

looked at my life, it became very clear that I managed my life in the city by utilizing my network in the city. It really is the way we navigate city life. This is valuable to the individual, but how is it useful for the community at large? The shadow tie is the social science equivalent of dark matter. It creates a force that's difficult to see but holds everything together.[9]

Michel Maffesoli drives the point home in his excellent work *The Time of the Tribes*.[10] As he documents the effects of postmodernism on urban groups, he states that tribes are "more than a residual category of social life, they are the central feature and key social fact of our own experience of everyday living."[11] He claims they now form an "underground centrality" to a city's life, pulse, and community.

This dark matter, or these loose connections, are often the real relational capital needed to see a movement spread through a city. Sociologist Rodney Stark notes that one of the major reasons that the early Christian movement was able to spread so quickly through the vast expanses of the Roman Empire was its decentralized, relational networks that enabled the gospel to spread organically from one group to another in natural, holistic, and integrated ways.[12] In other words, the early followers of Jesus were able to bring together their existing networks, norms,

and values in such a way that when they were converted to Jesus, something arose in their social experience and the kingdom of God flourished and moved through their midst. I believe that the rise of urban tribes today presents a unique opportunity for the church to capitalize on these networks, to regain social and kingdom capital for the renewal of our cities and world.

As followers of Jesus, we know that when we come together in his name, he is in our midst. We also know that he has promised to be with us always, even till the end of the age. What would happen if believers were able to organize their tribes—their networks, norms, and values—around the teachings and mission of Jesus and see a resurgence of the gospel spread from tribe to tribe?

ORGANIZING TRIBES?

This begs the question: *How does an urban tribe form*? How do you start something that is in its nature organic? Typically, people gather around ideas and needs, and over time become a functioning tribe. Seth Godin states, "A tribe is a group of people connected to one another, connected to a leader, and connected to an idea. . . . A group needs only two things to be a tribe: a shared interest and a way to communicate."[13] He goes on to say, "Leaders, on the other hand, don't care very much for organizational structure or the official blessing of whatever factory they work

for. They use passion and ideas to lead people, as opposed to using threats and bureaucracy to manage them."[14] Consequently, one of the simplest ways we have been able to form "missional tribes" at our church is by organizing people around need and passion.

The needs of the world are visible all around us, and people in today's culture are taking their own initiative to respond. Philanthropy is a new cultural value. From the (red) campaign to community service, from serving the poor to redeeming the inner city, from green movements to sustainable business, people are longing to be a part of something greater than themselves. Richard Rohr says, "Our ordinary lives are given an extraordinary significance when we accept that our lives are about something larger. I do not need to be the whole play or even understand the full script. It is enough to know that I have been chosen to be one actor on the stage. I need only play my part as well as I can."[15] Nearly everyone is passionate about something, and when followers of Jesus center their lives on a kingdom cause, powerful things can happen.

Empowering people around need and mission not only nurtures the communal nature of tribes, but it takes the kingdom of God outside of the walls of the church and into the networks, norms, and values of our culture. The kingdom begins to spread in small but potent ways and work its way itself into the social fabric of our world, doing a powerful work of renewal. Gathering people around mission lets the heart of God intersect with the people of God and the needs of the world, releasing the kingdom into the culture.

Let me give an example. A couple of years ago, a few people in our community noticed that the commodification of Valentine's Day was getting worse and worse. As believers with a heart for the city, they started to think about whom this was hurting the most. They realized that for women who have been victims of abusive relationships, this was probably a day of great pain. These two leaders, one an accountant and another a designer, went to the local battered women's shelter and asked if they could do something special for these women to redeem the day. This idea of redemption spread from group to group, until the plan began to take shape. They would partner with all the people in their networks who worked in the fashion industry to get sample clothing and products from the top designers in the city and work with makeup artists and hairstylists to get cosmetics and product. They networked with chefs to make first-class food, children's workers to stage a show for the women's kids, and a host of people to be willing to serve. They rented a loft in Soho and put on one of the most impressive displays of serving you can imagine. Women were weeping as they got to choose new clothes from the city's top designers for job interviews. Tears

were running down their cheeks as leading make-up artists gave them consultations on presenting themselves and looking their best. They were literally speechless as they were served incredible food and pampered for the first time in years. People from outside of our church community, through all of these overlapping networks, homeless, refugees, immigrants, and countless other needs. Organizing community around mission ensures that the kingdom of God is not an afterthought or an option for the spiritually mature, but the heart of what it means to follow Jesus.

PHILANTHROPY IS A NEW CULTURAL VALUE.

got involved and donated time, resources, advertising, and space to make this night a reality. In fact, a new tribe has formed that puts on this event every year and meets to plan and dream and act on behalf of these women. This is a kind of social capital, infused with love and vision, that when released into the culture at large, becomes *kingdom capital* with the potential to transform people, communities, and the world.

In our church community, we have people gathered around helping the poor, working with victims of sex trafficking, renewing the arts, raising missional families, caring for a specific neighborhood or the environment, serving underprivileged children,

THE NEW HELLENIZATION

Is it really possible to renew culture through missional urban tribes? I believe so. When Alexander the Great conquered the world, the genius of his influence was the idea of Hellenization. He sent functioning Greek communities into a conquered region to spread the values, customs, language, arts, and ideas of Hellenistic culture. Over the course of time, this Greek influence spread, so that regions were not just captured militarily, they were captured and transformed culturally. The Greeks were so effective in their task that many Jewish people even forgot their language and had to translate the Hebrew Scriptures into Greek, while New

Testament writers also penned their stories and letters in Greek. Alexander's real genius wasn't military power; it was his power to capture the imagination of his world.

In many ways this is what Jesus called his disciples to do and still calls us to do today: to go into our communities as functioning missional tribes, modeling, loving, reclaiming, and recovering cultural capital for his kingdom and the world. After all, what did Jesus create, but a missional tribe: a group of people from different backgrounds, centering their networks, norms, and values around him, bringing peace and renewal and hope wherever they went. They were a city on a hill, the light of the world, and as these groups went from city to city, they "kingdomized" their world through love and justice and mission and truth.

Several years later, Anna is still in the city, and she has found her tribe. Anna has quite a broken past: addiction, alcoholism, promiscuity, and low self-esteem, which led to abusive relationships and destructive behavior. But God is redeeming these broken things in her life and using them as her mission. She is gathering around others with similar stories to bring hope and healing to those still finding their way. She is a part of a team that counsels battered women when they are admitted to hospitals and does makeover nights for victims of sex trafficking. If you ask her if she still wants to be an actress, she will say, "Not really. I don't need to act to tell a story. I am part of a better story in the world—the redemptive drama of God who has invited me to join him in the renewal of all things. I have found my role in the story and am living it with joy."

Two thousand years later, Jesus is still forming his tribe, and he invites us in. May we hear his call, organize our lives around his needs and passion, and bring his kingdom into the networks, norms, and values of our lives.

Jon Tyson *is the pastor of Trinity Grace Church in New York City, a community of neighborhood churches committed to joining God in the renewal of all things. He also collaborates with cityparish .org, a movement of urban churches seeking to reclaim, redeem, and renew the world's global cities. Originally from Adelaide, Australia, he lives on the Upper West Side with his wife and children and can often be found listening to jazz downtown, reveling in the gifts of music and espresso.*

END NOTES

1 Robert D. Putnam, *Bowling Alone: The Collapse and Revival of American Community* (New York: Simon & Schuster, 2000).

2 See summary by Robert Putnam at http://www.bowlingalone.com.

3 Putnam, *Bowling Alone*, 19.

4 Ibid., 404.

5 Ethan Watters, *Urban Tribes: A Generation Redefines Friendship, Family and Commitment* (New York: Bloomsbury, 2003).

6 Howard Fineman, "Our New Tribes," in *Newsweek*, January 26, 2009, 61.

7 Ibid.

8 Ethan Watters, "Urban Tribes and Social Dark Matter," transcript of presentation on May 15, 2004 by Heath Row at *Fast Company* website at http://www.fastcompany.com/blog/heath-row/urban-tribes-and-social-dark-matter.

9 Ibid.

10 Michel Maffesoli, *The Time of the Tribes: The Decline of Individualism in Mass Society*, English Translation (London: Sage Publications, 1996).

11 Ibid., Foreword.

12 Rodney Stark, *The Rise of Christianity: A Sociologist Reconsiders History* (Princeton: Princeton University Press, 1996).

13 Seth Godin, *Tribes: We Need You to Lead Us* (New York: Penguin Group, 2008), 1.

14 Ibid., 22.

15 Richard Rohr with John Bookser Feister, *Jesus' Plan for a New World: The Sermon on the Mount* (Cincinnati: St. Anthony Messenger Press, 1996).

Americans are right that the bonds of our communities have withered, and we are right to fear that this transformation has very real costs.

ROBERT PUTNAM

The Bible tells us that the Christian is in the world, and that there he or she must remain. Christians have not been created in order to separate themselves from, or to live aloof from, the world.... The Christian community must never be a closed body.

JACQUES ELLUL

A tribe is a group of people connected to one another, connected to a leader, and connected to an idea.... A group needs only two things to be a tribe: a shared interest and a way to communicate.

SETH GODIN

RENEWING CITIES THROUGH MISSIONAL TRIBES

—

YOUR TRIBE

DISCUSS

—

Individualism reigns. We order customized coffee drinks, drive to work alone, and often communicate with others primarily through email and the Internet. Nevertheless, we still have our unique "tribes"—webs of relationships where we find community. These include mothers' playgroups, neighborhood friends, sports groups (e.g., golf, tennis, skiing, working out at the gym), workplace associates, etc.

DISCUSSION STARTERS

What is your primary "tribe"?

What brings your tribe together?

Do you find the most meaningful relationships in your life within this tribe or somewhere else?

PARTICIPATION IN LOCAL VOLUNTARY GROUPS

	%YES	%NO
Local church, synagogue, mosque or temple	46.1	53.9
Local social club or charitable organization	24.4	75.6
Community group or neighborhood association	16.0	84.0
Local sports league	16.0	84.0
Local youth group, such as scouts or YMCA	15.7	84.3
Some other local group	10.8	89.2

Source: Pew Internet and American Life Project: "Social Isolation and New Technology" by Keith Hampton, Lauren Sessions, Eun Ja Her, Lee Rainie, November 4, 2009 at http://pewinternet.org/Reports/2009/18--Social-Isolation-and-New-Technology.aspx.

THE EFFECTIVENESS OF SMALL GROUPS

DEBATE

Split the group into two sides* and spend twenty minutes debating the issue:

Do you agree with Jon Tyson's concern regarding community programs within the church?

Record your thoughts on each position on pages 52-53.

Use the following debate starters to guide your time.

In recent years, many churches have launched small groups ministries. Sometimes these replace Sunday school programs as the primary environment for Bible study. More often than not, the goal is to cultivate community among believers. Yet, Jon Tyson worries that these attempts to program community inside the church are disconnected from the norms, values, and networks of our everyday lives. They can often feel forced and unnatural, and they rarely help us engage our culture at large.

Do you agree?

DEBATE STARTERS

What is the purpose of small groups?

Is it possible to program relationships or community?

Can Christians find meaningful community in organic, missional tribes?

What are the strengths of encouraging missional tribes?

Even if you don't agree with the side you are representing, consider and offer the best arguments for your position. Be respectful.

—

YES

Small groups ministries, as they are often implemented, don't breed real community and are ineffective at helping Christians engage culture outside the church in a meaningful way.

THOUGHTS

—

NO

Small groups are the best way to help Christians find community, regardless of whether or not they connect to the norms, values, and other networks in our lives.

THOUGHTS

CHRISTIAN COMMUNITY

Have a few people in your group take turns reading this section aloud.

Then journal your thoughts on pages 56-57.

The book of Acts describes the early Christian community:

> They devoted themselves to the apostles' teaching and to fellowship, to the breaking of bread and to prayer. Everyone was filled with awe at the many wonders and signs performed by the apostles. All the believers were together and had everything in common. They sold property and possessions to give to anyone who had need. Every day they continued to meet together in the temple courts. They broke bread in their homes and ate together with glad and sincere hearts, praising God and enjoying the favor of all the people. And the Lord added to their number daily those who were being saved.
> – Acts 2:42–47

There are several dynamics at play here. First, the community was grounded in its faith in God (through studying the apostles' teaching, taking communion together, prayer, and worship). Second, it was a community that loved one another—they made sure that no one went without. Third, they met in both large venues (in the temple courts) and small gatherings (in homes). And finally, their community made an impact on their wider culture as more

people became Christians and joined the community.

All of this seems to underscore the twofold purpose of Christian community: existing for the benefit of one another, but also existing for the benefit of those outside of the community.

REFLECTION STARTERS

Spend a few minutes journaling your thoughts to the three questions below. Then, share your reflections with the group.

Is your immediate Christian community (house church, small group, Sunday school class, Bible study, etc.) better at serving the needs of those within your group or outside of it? Where can it improve?

Christian community is never easy. Dietrich Bonhoeffer wrote in *Life Together*: "He who loves his dream of community more than the Christian community itself becomes a destroyer of the latter." What do you think he means? What unrealistic expectations do we place on community?

How can our communities more effectively benefit or bless those in our wider culture?

JOURNAL

JOURNAL

A COMMUNITY OF MISSION

CONCLUDE

We live in an individualistic culture. The church is not immune from this reality and often has a difficult time helping people find genuine community that both strengthens their faith and makes a difference in culture. But both are necessary for living out the mission of God in our world.

How do friends in your social circles and workplace view the church, and how might your own Christian community change their perspective?

GET AN OUTSIDER'S PERCEPTION

PREPARE FOR NEXT GATHERING

It's important to understand the perceptions that most people in our culture have about the Christian community. Before your next group gathering, make it a point to have a conversation with a non-Christian friend about his or her perceptions. Tell that person that you're genuinely interested in an honest opinion. Then simply listen. Explore questions such as: What do you think of Christians? Do you believe that churches are good for society? Would you ever attend a church? Why or why not? What could Christians and/or the church do that would be a benefit for you?

PREPARING FOR YOUR CULTURE SHAPING PROJECT

In the next few weeks, your group will take part in a project together to apply what you are learning and discussing. It's important that you complete this project before your last gathering. Three options for what your group can do have been recommended on pages 96–97. All of them require some planning and preparation. Take a few minutes now to read the options and discuss which one best suits your group. You don't have to make a decision this week, but you need to get the ball rolling and be prepared to make a decision and start planning at your next group meeting.

We are the people of the parenthesis—at the end of one era but not quite at the beginning of the next one. Maps no longer fit the new territories. In order to make sense of it all, we must cultivate a vision.

JEAN HOUSTON

Christendom has done away with Christianity without being quite aware of it.

SØREN KIERKEGAARD

A church which pitches its tents without constantly looking out for new horizons, which does not continually strike camp, is being untrue to its calling…. [We must] play down our longing for certainty, accept what is risky, and live by improvisation and experiment.

HANS KÜNG

POST-CHRISTENDOM MISSION

THE END OF CHRISTENDOM

Spend a few minutes sharing your thoughts with the group.

Christendom is a society where the majority of people profess Christianity and where the collective beliefs, customs, and values of the culture are guided by the Christian faith. Clearly then, as we have already explored, contemporary American culture can no longer be described by the term *Christendom*. And the trend away from Christendom only grows. What are the primary factors that have brought about the end of Christendom in the West?

DISCUSSION STARTERS

Why is American culture no longer guided by Christian values?

What role does the church now play in the public square?

Can the church still hope to attract people to its community by becoming more relevant, or is another approach needed to engage culture at large?

—

CHARACTERISTICS OF TWO DISTINCT ERAS IN WESTERN CHURCH HISTORY

EARLY CHURCH (AD 30s to early 300s)	CHRISTENDOM (mid 300s to 1900s)
No dedicated chuch buildings	Buildings become central to the expression of the church
Church is often underground and persecuted	Church and state/political structures often connected
Decentralized, grassroots, organic movement	Institutional structure with hierarchical leadership
Church is on the margins of society	Church is perceived as central to society and surrounding culture
Influence on culture through missional, incarnational approach	Influence through exertion of power and attracting people to the church

Source: Adapted from Michael Frost and Alan Hirsch, The Shaping of Things to Come *(Peabody, Mass.: Hendrickson, 2003), p. 9.*

—

POST-CHRISTENDOM MISSION

WATCH

—

View Q Talk: Post-Christendom Mission by Alan Hirsch.

Record your thoughts on the talk on page 67.

If we now live in a post-Christian world, what should the church look like and how does the mission of the church adapt within this new context? Alan Hirsch is the founding director of Forge Mission Training Network and a sought-after speaker who travels the world to help Christians engage these questions.

At Q Austin, Alan challenged listeners to reconsider our mission within the post-Christian West. As a native of Australia, he brings a unique perspective to the American audience, beckoning us to embody a pioneering spirit as cross-cultural missionaries in our own culture

—

"In order to communicate the gospel meaningfully, the local church outreach picnic and service isn't going to cut it any longer. You're going to have to adopt a cross-cultural mission methodology in the Western context."

—

"In the attractional model, they've got to do the cross-cultural work to come to us. But, we as missionaries ought to do the cross-cultural work to go to them."

—

"Sixty percent of your country, for whatever reason, will not go to the attractional church. So what are we going to do about people who find themselves within the 60 percent? What does church look like for them?"

—

"If we all persist in producing what we're currently producing, we are perfectly designed to achieve what we're currently achieving now."

THOUGHTS

A NEW APPROACH

DEBATE

Split the group into two sides* and spend fifteen minutes debating the issue:

Do you agree or disagree that there must be new, pioneering ways of doing church in a post-Christian culture?

Record your thoughts on each position on pages 70-71.

Use the following debate starters to guide your time.

Alan Hirsch asserts that the attractional or church growth model of church—creating relevant environments that reach people who are within the church's cultural orbit—will never be able to reach approximately 60 percent of Americans. While he affirms the work of churches that are effective at reaching the 40 percent of Americans who are not far removed from church culture, he believes that there must be new, pioneering ways of doing church in order to thrive in a post-Christian culture.

Do you agree there must be new, pioneering ways of doing church in a post-Christian culture?

DEBATE STARTERS

Would you consider your church attractional and, if so, what kind of people is it best at reaching?

Do you think the idea that attitudes toward church in America aren't far behind those in Australia and Europe is valid or overstated? Why?

What will it take for the gospel to be communicated in a meaningful way to those who are far outside of the church's cultural orbit?

How would the ministries of a church change to reach someone who is hostile or just apathetic to Christianity?

Even if you don't agree with the side you are representing, consider and offer the best arguments for your position. Be respectful.

—

YES

Many churches should abandon the attractional approach and radically innovate their approach in order to reach a growing majority of Americans.

THOUGHTS

—

NO

The problem is that we don't have enough churches that have attractive and relevant programs to meet people's needs.

THOUGHTS

REACHING MODEL-CAR RACERS

Have a few people in the group take turns reading this section aloud.

Then journal your thoughts on page 75.

Let's explore this distinction between an "attractional" and an "incarnational" approach a little more. In Alan Hirsch and Michael Frost's book, *The Shaping of Things to Come*, they offer an example.

Some time ago I (Michael) was watching my daughter play soccer in a local park. Next to the field was an asphalted area where a group of model-car enthusiasts had set up a track and were using remote controls to race their cars against one another's. The constant buzz of the miniature motors caught our attention and we wandered over to watch what they were doing. We soon realized we had encountered a lost suburban tribe. Everyone looked the same. They all wore tight black jeans and checkered flannel shirts. They wore baseball caps with car manufacturers' logos on them. They had parked their cars—virtually all drove pickups—beside the track, and their wives or girlfriends sat in one of the truckbeds talking and laughing loudly. It was a tribe in every sense of the word— dress code, language, culture, and customs. We learned that once a month on a Sunday morning they met to race each other, to discuss the latest designs in model cars, and to drink and laugh and build community.

If the nearby church decided that this suburban tribe needed to hear about the saving work of Christ, how would they reach them? The attractional church would hold special services for model-car racers. It would design an excellent flyer explaining that Jesus loves model-car enthusiasts, and they would place one under the windshield wipers of each pickup. It would try to find a recently converted model-car enthusiast and have him share his testimony one Sunday morning. The attractional church would seek to do anything it could to draw the car-racing fraternity into its building. This might even work if you're dealing with a localized community with some geographic proximity to the church building. But a car club community usually draws people from a very large geographic area. The model-car club is probably a citywide community, and its members probably drive great distances to come to its monthly meetings. They are not drawn together by some geographic proximity, but by a commonly held interest. And to complicate matters further, they meet on Sunday mornings!

The attractional church is stuck! Even though it has a close-knit community of people (likely non-churchgoers) right outside its door, it has no mechanism for sharing Christ with them. Since they (the car club members) are not likely to turn up at the church service one Sunday (doesn't the attractional church love stories of people miraculously turning up at the church service searching for meaning and purpose!), the only way to share Christ's love with them must be to go to them. It would be a decidedly incarnational choice if a few

members of a local church, so moved by compassion for the car enthusiasts right across the road, chose to buy a model car and join the club! This would be the kind of thinking and acting we're talking about. If the spirit of our missionary God were to sweep through such a church, we don't doubt that the church itself might buy a few model cars and commission some of its members to miss the morning service so they can fully enter into the community of the car club. By racing cars and repairing cars, they could earn the right of relationship to share their thoughts on life and their love for Jesus. This is the incarnational church in action. If a few car racers came into a relationship with Christ, they should not be encouraged to leave the club and join the church. Rather, a home church could be established, and the brand-new Christian car enthusiasts could worship God in the context of their tribal identity. (Hendrickson, 2003, pp. 42–43)

REFLECTION STARTERS

Spend a few minutes journaling your thoughts to the two questions below. Then, share your reflections with the group.

What are some examples of tribes in your city that the attractional model of church will likely never reach?

How can Jesus' incarnation serve as the example of how we engage those in need of his love?

JOURNAL

WE ARE ALL MISSIONARIES

CONCLUDE

The current model of many growing American churches is successful at reaching people who are not that far removed from Christian subculture. But in order to reach an increasingly post-Christian culture, a new pioneering spirit must be born. Will the next generation of Christians have the courage to begin seeing themselves as missionaries?

How does viewing yourself as a missionary change the way you interact with others in your spheres of influence?

—

TAKE ON A MISSION MIND-SET

PREPARE FOR NEXT GATHERING

—

Your church probably supports missionaries who are serving among people groups in places that are not very open to Christianity. Spend some time this week finding out more about what these missionaries do. Read their websites, sign up for their newsletters, or communicate with one of them if you can. What kind of approach are they taking to build relationships and engage their culture? How have they been successful? Where have they met barriers? Begin to see their work as an example of how we too can be missionaries in our culture.

Spend the final portion of your time together discussing your culture shaping project.

PLANNING THE CULTURE SHAPING PROJECT

You'll need to make a decision by the end of this gathering since what you do will likely require planning. Your project needs to take place before your last group gathering and it should be something that everyone can participate in. You can review the suggestions given on pages 96–97. It may be difficult to find total agreement among the group, but try to establish some consensus by talking through the advantages and disadvantages of all suggestions. Don't be afraid to think creatively and challenge yourselves. You're not limited by the suggestions included in this study, but you'll want to undertake something that will help you apply what you've been learning. Make a decision and solidify action steps before you conclude.

Everyone thinks of changing the world, but no one thinks of changing himself.

LEO TOLSTOY

I am only one, but I am one. I cannot do everything, but I can do something. And I will not let what I cannot do interfere with what I can do.

EDWARD EVERETT HALE

If you can't feed a hundred people, then feed just one.

MOTHER TERESA

GROUP GATHERING FOUR

WHY WE CAN'T CHANGE
THE WORLD

—

THE DAUNTING CHALLENGE

DISCUSS

—

During the last three gatherings, your group has discussed some enormous obstacles to the growth of the Christian message in our culture: secularization and pluralism, individualism, and our increasing inability to be relevant to a culture that is no longer interested in our beliefs.

DISCUSSION STARTERS

Do these challenges seem daunting?

Amid all your daily concerns, how often do you think about your mission in a post-Christian culture?

What are some examples of churches or Christians who you believe are meeting these challenges well?

SIX PERCEPTIONS OF CHRISTIANITY

PERCEPTION	OUTSIDERS Ages 26 to 29
Antihomosexual	91%
Judgmental	87%
Hypocritical	85%
Sheltered (old-fashioned, out of touch with reality)	78%
Too political	75%
Proselytizers (insensitive to others, not genuine)	70%

Source: "Q commissioned research study by the Barna Group." Further statistics available in the book, UnChristian.

—

WHY WE CAN'T CHANGE THE WORLD

WATCH

—

View Q Talk: Why We Can't Change the World by Andy Crouch.

Record your thoughts on page 85.

We're encouraged when we see others casting huge visions and undertaking significant initiatives; we're inspired to go out and do something that will change the world. But what if we've gotten it wrong when it comes to how the world is changed? At Q New York, Andy Crouch offered a different perspective that is guaranteed to test our assumptions.

Andy Crouch is the author of *Culture Making: Recovering Our Creative Calling*, winner of *Christianity Today's* 2009 Book Award for Christianity and Culture. He is also a senior editor at Christianity Today International, a member of the editorial board of *Books & Culture*, and a senior fellow of the International Justice Mission's IJM Institute.

—

"The best possible news we could hear is that we are not the ones who will change the world."

—

"The two biggest culture making events in history did not start in the center; they started at the edges."

—

"God steps in on behalf of his people precisely at the moment when all their success has evaporated. God intervenes in the world precisely at the moment where everything seems lost, at precisely the place where no one wants to go, and on behalf of people no one believes can do anything of significance."

—

"If God is the subject of transforming culture, then we are not agents of cultural transformation. We are the patients . . . those who suffer and are being healed."

THOUGHTS

—

HOW THE WORLD IS CHANGED

DEBATE

—

Split the group into two sides*
and spend fifteen minutes
debating the issue:

How will God transform our
culture?

Record your thoughts on each
position on pages 88-89.

Use the following debate starters
to guide your time.

We often believe that the world can be changed when we gain power. If we can just elect the right people and put in place the right laws, then we can change culture. Or, if we can just control the media, or the corporate world, or the educational system, then we could influence culture in the right direction. But Andy Crouch presents an alternative perspective. God is the only one who changes the world. (We would all agree.) But God often uses the weak, the powerless, those on the margins to do it. (This can be either difficult or encouraging to hear depending on your circumstances.)

What do you think? How will God transform our culture?

DEBATE STARTERS

Were Andy Crouch's examples of the exodus and resurrection compelling or not?

Are there other examples from Scripture where God used those in power to change the world?

Can you cite examples in culture where a top-down approach has been effective?

Are we too focused on a short-term perspective of making a difference? How can God use our suffering and failures to change culture?

Even if you don't agree with the side you are representing, consider and offer the best arguments for your position. Be respectful.

—

YES

We must adopt a bottom-up mind-set; our failures and powerlessness place us in the precise position God wants us to be in order to transform the world.

THOUGHTS

NO

A top-down perspective is more realistic; those who hold political, economic, and cultural power will continue to have the greatest influence in our culture.

THOUGHTS

A COMMUNITY GOD USES TO CHANGE THE WORLD

REFLECT

Have a few people in the group take turns reading this section aloud.

Then journal your thoughts on pages 92-93.

One "success story" in particular bears mentioning. You may have heard of William Wilberforce, the leader of the abolitionist movement in England, who has been written about extensively and was profiled in the film *Amazing Grace* (2006). Wilberforce had political power in England and several wealthy individuals underwrote his cause. Nevertheless, it took over forty years of hard work and suffering for him to abolish slavery and make a difference in culture. And few people appreciate the depth of community that surrounded Wilberforce and his cause.

Wilberforce and his friends lived five miles outside of London in an area known as Clapham Common for over forty years. The Clapham Circle of the late 1700s and early 1800s in England didn't just happen though. It was an intentional choice these friends made to live in proximity to one another and to share life over the long haul. People gravitated toward Clapham because they shared a common vision. They didn't just socialize, but had a deep, kindred connection that was foundational for all that they would do together.

Ultimately, the friends within the Clapham community were attracted and bound to one another out of their commitment to serve others. Over seventy social reforms are credited to the work of this circle of friends, including slavery abolition, improving the living and working conditions of the poor, and establishing the first animal humane society. This community did not exist for themselves—as beneficial as that was—they also existed for the wider community.

Our call as a Christian community is to be a light—not simply a bunch of small lights in all the dark corners of the world—but a communal light that provides a picture to the world of what a loving, sacrificial, countercultural community is. As Stanley Haurwas and Will Willimon put it:

> The world needs the church, not to help the world run more smoothly or to make the world a better and safer place for Christians to live. Rather, the world needs the church because, without the church, the world does not know who it is. The only way for the world to know that it is being redeemed is for the church to point to the Redeemer by being a redeemed people. (*Resident Aliens*, Abingdon, 1989, p. 94)

REFLECTION STARTERS

Spend a few minutes journaling your thoughts to the three questions below. Then, share your reflections with the group.

How has the Christian community that you participate in defined its mission?

How do you work together toward that mission?

How would you define success for your community?

JOURNAL

JOURNAL

CHANNELS OF GOD'S GRACE

CONCLUDE

Only God changes the world, and he has already done so through the redemptive and restorative work of Jesus Christ. We make a difference in our culture when we ourselves are recipients of that grace—sharing in Christ's suffering and resurrection. And that involves risk, failure, pain, and often the death of our own dreams in order to be channels of God's message to our world.

What suffering and failure in your life can God use for his mission in our world?

—

CULTURE SHAPING PROJECT

—

Your primary assignment is to undertake your culture shaping project before your next gathering. Be intentional about setting aside time to prepare for and execute your project so that you can discuss it when you next meet. Project options follow on pages 96–97.

CULTURE SHAPING PROJECT

IDEAS FOR GROUP PROJECT

Your group has been discussing our mission in a new post-Christian culture. Now you have an opportunity to take what you are learning and do something together. Be sure to plan this group project early and undertake it before your final group gathering. Following are three options you might consider.

Option One: Change Your Community

What are the biggest injustices that exist in your own neighborhood and city? Are there working poor that are neglected? Is adequate health care available to everyone? Are the public schools in need of assistance? Is the natural environment being abused? The list of potential issues could go on. As a group, research the problems that your local community faces and decide to make a difference by simply being available to help. Start by spending time one day volunteering at a local school, helping a nonprofit organization, or simply picking up trash at a local park. See your service to the community as an integral part of being a missionary in your culture.

Option Two: Film Screening

Host a movie night where you invite non-Christian friends over to watch the documentary *Lord, Save Us From Your Followers*. After the film, have a conversation about the topics raised. What does the film portray about how others perceive Christians? How have the culture wars divided so many Americans and turned them off to Christianity? What should Christians respond? Be intentional about listening to what outsiders think. For more information, visit: www.lordsaveusthemovie.com.

Option Three: Host a Party!

As a group, host a cookout or party at someone's house where each person invites several non-Christian friends in his or her sphere of influence. Feel free to use an event to guide the party (the Super Bowl, the 4th of July, New Year's Day, etc.). The key is to create an environment where others from your neighborhood, tribes, or cultural channels of influence can interact with those in your Christian community. You don't need an agenda for the party other than to cultivate relationships and create space for conversations and relationships to happen.

The main stimulus for the renewal of Christianity will come from the bottom and from the edge, from sectors of the Christian world that are on the margins.

HARVEY COX

Nothing is more difficult to carry out, nor more doubtful of success, nor more dangerous to handle, than achieving a new order of things.

NICCOLO MACHIAVELLI

Change is inevitable … adapting to change is unavoidable, it's how you do it that sets you together or apart.

WILLIAM MAPHOTO

OUR MISSION AS WORSHIP

EVALUATING THE PROJECT

DISCUSS

Over the past several weeks, you've been exposed to some new ideas. Your group has discussed and debated how these concepts might change the way you think about faith and culture. And you've worked on a group project together to begin considering how these ideas might change the way you live your lives. Spend some time evaluating what you learned during your group project.

DISCUSSION STARTERS

How difficult was it to undertake your group project?

Did you find any part of it uncomfortable or not helpful? Why?

What's the most important thing you learned during your group project?

How were you able to see your project as a way of becoming a missionary in your culture?

THOUGHTS

OUR WORSHIP

REFLECT

Have a few people in the group take turns reading this section aloud.

Then journal your thoughts on pages 104-105.

Israel was a community of faith that was supposed to make a difference in the world. In the midst of so many other nations that did not believe in God or follow his teachings, Israel was called to be a countercultural community offering an alternative way of life. But they simply weren't doing it. They ignored many of God's laws, took advantage of the poor, and other than the God they prayed to, their lives looked no different from anyone else's. So the prophet Isaiah roundly condemned them:

> Hear the word of the LORD,
>   you rulers of Sodom;
> listen to the instruction of our God,
>   you people of Gomorrah!
> "The multitude of your sacrifices—
>   what are they to me?" says the LORD.
> "I have more than enough of burnt offerings,
>   of rams and the fat of fattened animals;
> I have no pleasure
>   in the blood of bulls and lambs and goats.
> When you come to appear before me,
>   who has asked this of you,
>   this trampling of my courts?

Stop bringing meaningless offerings!
    Your incense is detestable to me.
New Moons, Sabbaths and convocations—
    I cannot bear your evil assemblies.
Your New Moon feasts and your appointed festivals
    I hate with all my being.
They have become a burden to me;
    I am weary of bearing them.
When you spread out your hands in prayer,
    I will hide my eyes from you;
even if you offer many prayers,
    I will not listen.
Your hands are full of blood."
– Isaiah 1:10–15

In light of such harsh words, Old Testament scholar John Goldingay offers some thoughts:

> Isaiah surveys every kind of worship the people offer—their sacramental rites, their gatherings in [God's] presence, their offerings, their celebrations, their prayer meetings. All of this they do with enthusiasm. But [God] hates it all. That applies not merely to outward acts such as sacrifice, but to all forms of worship, including prayer. Isaiah does not attack worship that is outwardly correct but not sincerely meant; this is not the antithesis he works with. He assumes that the people mean every hallelujah. His critique is rather that their enthusiastic worship of [God] is not matched by an enthusiastic living before [God] in everyday life. There is a

mismatch between their worship and their community life, not between their outward worship and inward attitude. (*Old Testament Theology Vol. Three: Israel's Life*, IVP Academic, 2009, p. 23)

REFLECTION STARTERS

Spend a few minutes journaling your thoughts to these questions, then share with the group.

Evangelical and liturgical churches alike are known for the extravagance of their worship (albeit in different ways). Could you ever imagine God hating your church's worship or ignoring your prayers because they are not matched by a lifestyle of mission within the community?

What do you think a prophet would say today to your community of faith? What can your Society Room group do to present an alternative way of life in your city?

JOURNAL

YOU ARE COMMISSIONED

CONCLUDE

How do you view your mission in culture differently as a result of this Q Society Room study?

What have you learned?

What will change about your lifestyle in the future?

What will you start doing?

What will you stop doing?

Spend the last fifteen minutes of your gathering praying as a group. In the New Testament, when the local church at Antioch sent off Paul and Barnabas as missionaries, they prayed, fasted, and laid hands on them (a symbolic gesture of commissioning someone for a specific role; Acts 13:1–3). As you pray, "commission" one another as missionaries in your neighborhoods, tribes, and channels of cultural influence. Ask God for patience, endurance, and courage to be his redemptive presence in culture. If you've never prayed in a group, don't let this intimidate you. Your prayers need not be elaborate or articulate. Simply talk to God. End your time by discussing how you will continue to encourage one another:

"Let us not grow weary in doing good, for at the proper time
we will reap a harvest if we do not give up."
– Galatians 6:9

Embrace your mission.

Share Your Thoughts

With the Author: Your comments will be forwarded to the author when you send them to *zauthor@zondervan.com*.

With Zondervan: Submit your review of this book by writing to *zreview@zondervan.com*.

Free Online Resources at

www.zondervan.com

Zondervan AuthorTracker: Be notified whenever your favorite authors publish new books, go on tour, or post an update about what's happening in their lives at www.zondervan.com/authortracker.

Daily Bible Verses and Devotions: Enrich your life with daily Bible verses or devotions that help you start every morning focused on God. Visit www.zondervan.com/newsletters.

Free Email Publications: Sign up for newsletters on Christian living, academic resources, church ministry, fiction, children's resources, and more. Visit www.zondervan.com/newsletters.

Zondervan Bible Search: Find and compare Bible passages in a variety of translations at www.zondervanbiblesearch.com.

Other Benefits: Register yourself to receive online benefits like coupons and special offers, or to participate in research.

ZONDERVAN.com/
AUTHORTRACKER

TABLE OF CONTENTS

ZONDERVAN

Engaging Post-Christian Culture Participant's Guide
Copyright © 2010 Q

Requests for information should be addressed to:

Zondervan, *Grand Rapids, Michigan 49530*

ISBN 978-0-310-32522-2

All Scripture quotations are taken from the Holy Bible, *Today's New International Version*™. *TNIV*®. Copyright © 2001, 2005 by Biblica, Inc.™ Used by permission of Zondervan. All rights reserved worldwide.

Any Internet addresses (websites, blogs, etc.) and telephone numbers printed in this book are offered as a resource. They are not intended in any way to be or imply an endorsement by Zondervan, nor does Zondervan vouch for the content of these sites and numbers for the life of this book.

All rights reserved. No part of this publication may be reproduced, stored in a retrieval system, or transmitted in any form or by any means—electronic, mechanical, photocopy, recording, or any other—except for brief quotations in printed reviews, without the prior permission of the publisher.

Published in association with Yates & Yates, www.yates2.com.

Printed in the United States of America

10 11 12 13 14 15 16 /DCI/ 32 31 30 29 28 27 26 25 24 23 22 21 20 19 18 17 16 15 14 13 12 11 10 9 8 7 6 5 4 3 2 1

MW01070658

—

ENGAGING POST-CHRISTIAN CULTURE: OUR MISSION IN A NEW CONTEXT

—

Q Society Room

A Group Learning Experience

Five Group Gatherings

NORTON HERBST AND GABE LYONS

ZONDERVAN.com/
AUTHORTRACKER
follow your favorite authors